WICCA
TOOLS
FOR BEGINNERS

THE COMPLETE GUIDE
Candle, Herbs, Crystals, Tarot,
Essential Oils and Altar
How to Start Guidebook

DAPHNE BROOKS

WICCA TOOLS FOR BEGINNERS

TABLE OF CONTENTS

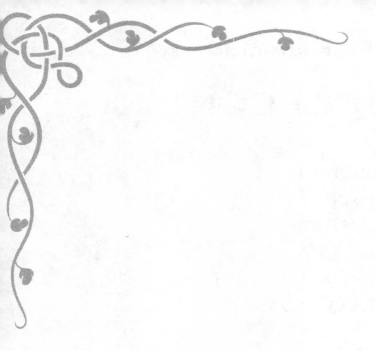

WICCA TOOLS FOR BEGINNERS

INTRODUCTION

O ver the years, the eyes of many have been opened to the most important truth of the century: we are all part of more substantial nature. And Wicca has a more significant role to play in it. Many things and events have tried to stifle this knowledge from the earth, but any real idea or religion has its way of returning to the surface.

There was a time when being a Wicca, which had a different name at that time, was an offense. But the present world has made it glaring that we can excel. Being a reviving culture or religion, a lot of people have made several suggestions through books, blogs, vlogs, and so many other media. These suggestions now make it hard for a new convert to enjoy the beauty of this religion.

In light of that, this book is aimed at guiding you through the different aspects of Wicca. As much as there is complex information everywhere. It had been simplified, and the knowledge is gleaned not only from personal experiences but from the knowledge and the skills of sages.

Written with you in mind, this book has been set to enlighten you, and that journey starts now.

CHAPTER - I

WHAT IS WICCA?

Wicca is culture modelled after the traditions in existence before the coming of Christianity into Ireland, Scotland, and Wales.

You can call it having a deep connection to the nature around us. It is appreciating things like the sunrise, sunset, or the little things around us. You might find joy in such thing as the way the morning dew is balanced on the petals of a flower.

In essence, Wicca is when one finds joys in the healing of others through natural means, seeking or protecting the natural things. It might even be when you have the desire to teach others about the intricacy of the naturalness of life.

ORIGIN OF WICCA

To take a more in-depth look at Wicca is to firstly understand that the processes defined up there had been at the pre--Christianity era. They have been used in the healing of people and had been used to improved several medical knowledge. However, unlike Christianity, many of these great understandings were not thoroughly documents.

Thus, when Christianity entered these high countries of the United Kingdom, it was easy to blot out some information. In reality, the word Wicca actually was the initial way of referring to witches at those times. However, when nomenclature moved from town to town, there was a shift in the pronunciation, making the name change from what it had been known for.

In fact, through the help of archaeologists, it is believed that this belief system emanated from the worship of Hunter god and a fertility goddess by the Palaeolithic people. These archaeologists traced their existence to about 30,000 years ago. Their discovery was made through the study of such things as cave paintings. The painting depicted a man who had a head of a stag and a pregnant woman in a circle created by eleven people. It is no longer news that a lot of information had been lost in the Christianity era, but many people have made several deductions and cold calculation that has helped in restricting the system. Thus, it can be concluded that Wicca is focused on the beliefs in the worship of the god and goddess. Anyone with the knowledge of Wicca is prone to study more about herbs and have a wide range of education in lines of medicine. In the days of predating Christianity, many witches were among the Shaman.

In ancient history, there was a sort of respect accorded Wiccans because witchcraft was regarded as a craft of the wise. One primary reason was that they were tuned to nature and had a vast knowledge of herbs and medicine, making them a very essential part of the survival of the villages or communities they reside in.

Because of their understanding of how human was just a part of the whole elements of nature, they have a way of reminding people of this salient point: humans were not superior to other aspects of life but are simply a part of the whole process. Thus, they always tend to help in the creation of balance and equilibrium of life. There is every assurance that the modern man has lost this value and have placed a higher value on the superiority of the existence of humans.

And we can clearly see this in the recent happenings around us including the ecological disasters around us as well the extinction of individual animals because of the human greed and desire for material wealth. This problem has its consequence; the eventual destruction of some unique animals or insects might lead to the extinction of the human species.

The past hundred years have unfortunately painted a bad image of witches. For some reason, they have been regarded as evil, unrighteous, and heathen. These misconceptions, however, emanated from centuries into the coming of Christianity.

When the medieval church began in the 15 century, certain myths were propagated among people, especially followers of this religion. The underlying message was that their faith was filled with evil and oppressive methods. Their mind was warped to believe they have been using diabolical means into the creation of balance. In other words, their servitude and reverence of nature were regarded as service to devils and demons. The missionary projected fear on the mind of people and made them suspicious of their gods because many of them were regarded as demon-filled deities. In fact, tales and imaginations were built around witches as wicked people.

The result, thereof, was that they were able to convert people through their fear. Not far from the coming of Christianity, there was the influx of medical science, which further made people have disregard for nature-based worship. Medical science, however, allowed people to have a standardized study of the human body, thus disregarding the potency of nature-based worship. The studies that had been carried out on several occasions were done by men, who were oblivious to many of the many problems faced by women.

This ignorance was one of the tools used by the church. Several of the missionaries were really vast in the knowledge of science and could easily fault the knowledge of the witches. The credence they got made it easy for the church to seem superior and this proved their erroneous beliefs as right, giving their witch hunt credibility.

The misinformation further went on to hold a lot of

people bound that it was easy to stop some traditions that many are yearning for its existence today. Looking at the glimpse of some of these traditions has proved itself to something the world needs today, but the knowledge is just limited. Now, to further understand these traditions by juxtaposing events with one another, Wicca started.

11

 The adoption of the name, however, came in to avoid the numerous persecution that came with the name with. This psychology even went as far as those that weren't Christians at that time.

This hideous image of witches remained in the series of events that have been enunciated movies and books. Many of the entertainment had tried to depict witches evil. To a large extent, this superstition had crossed several centuries and have found a resting place in the heart of several people on a day like.

To avoid the numerous persecution, harassment, as well as the misinformation linked to the name witch, the group decide to remain known as Wicca.

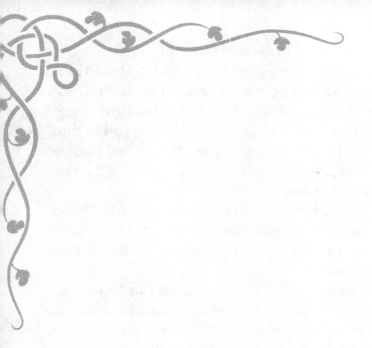

WICCA TOOLS FOR BEGINNERS

CHAPTER - 2
Candle

A candle is a tool used in harnessing the power of fire to cause change. In other words, it is an essential element for any transformation process. A better way to look at this tool is to see it functioning as regular fire. Anything touched by fire will definitely transform in one form or the other.

For the case of a candle, fire melts its wax. In other cases, it brings changes to inorganic materials and transforms them into ashes. Hard metals, on the other hand, are softened by fire, which gives it the ability to be forged into anything you want. More so, with it, the liquid is transformed into gas. On the other hand, it can help in the solid or liquid or fragile objects, which makes it easy for you to get a substantial or fried egg from the fragile one. Cake, an example of its solidifying power, is one that has been created for the heating up of several liquid materials.

Fire again can eradicate darkness from a place. Since the existence of humans, the discovery of fire has hel-

ped in many ways. Of the several beautiful things about fire is the desire to understand its power. Several bodies have sought out ways to understand and harness their power. Among the many people ready to appreciate its power, Wicca has taken a forefront in trying to harness its energy into a transformative function. So far, they have gotten an excellent result for it, which enable them to classify the candle as one of the most essential tools. From tradition, the candle had played a significant role in its transformative ability.

Below, you will get a good grasp of how to refocus the power of candle into your transformative process or desire.

STEP I: DETERMINATION OF THE DESIRED GOAL

Just as you would do other magical workings, there is a great need to place a higher focus on your goal. For with it, you can quickly achieve any other aspect of the process. Some tips have worked for others in helping you focus on your magical goal.

Specificity: Don't generalize. This will make your desire seem haphazard. Instead, focus on the need at hand and redirect your focus on that your desire.

14

Pragmaticism: Let your desire be such that is attainable. Push aside your fantasy aside and let reality be in play as you make your wish.

Ethics: Another thing you must keep in mind when making a request through a candle or other forms of power is that you must be ethical. Never let it be again freewill for this has its own consequences.

Positivity: When your mind is attuned to positivity, you have a higher chance of using positive words, which should be a real method of making your desire known. In other words, ensure you stay far from the 'not' statements, e.g., 'do not.' Cannot etc.

Target per Time: When you have a bigger goal, it is always advisable that you have a way of breaking it down into achievable target.

Now that you have these tips at hand, you can go on to write your goal, preferably in a single sentence. 'For example, I need extra income for the payment of the electric bill or ' I seek protection from harm when I travel.'

STEP 2: DESIGNING OF SPELL

Once your goal has been created, the next step is to find the right spell that fits the candle method of prayer. As it is with any spell making, there must be an under-standing of how complex or simple the desire is. Now, in the case of such things as electricity bills, you have to use the basic candle-magic spell. All that is required of you is to simply visualize your goal and release your energy through the lighten candle.

Thus, the things needed for the designing of the candle are simple. All you need to do is to get your candle and place it in its holder, some oils for the dressing of the candles, and probably some herbs or spice to make the power increased.

After it is done, the next step is relatively simple. You will chant to raise the energy of that place. There are several chants online that can help you in creating things. If you're not comfortable with that, you can use your book of shadows, which would be discussed later. Well, if you decide to go on the way of creating on your own, the only rule is to ensure it has meaning. Some people prefer to make it rhyme, making it easy to re-member.

Now, if you are such that will later create spell as a result of your moon signs and planetary hour, you can also check that out.

STEP 3: GATHER YOUR COMPONEN-TS

In the selection of your components, ensure they are

aligned with your goal. There are several colors for several reasons, and you don't want to overlook it when it has been discussed in the next few pages. To augment your candle, you will need to get herbs and spice to up your energy level, and those that actually align with your goal. In the case of money spell as discussed earlier, you only one candle, the holder, and some oils as well as your herbs and spice in lending power.

Well, in selecting your components, it is best you use certain criteria. Well, since we have started with the example of money-making, we will place the focus on how your selection can be made here. This method can work for other things too, nonetheless.

Your Virgin Candle: In selecting a candle for your spell, your instinct and knowledge will always play a role for you. If you're not too sure, you can always check out the list of colors and the things they do.

The Color of the Candle Holder: In the case of this money spell, the gold can be chosen as gold depicts wealth. It might actually not be a real gold-coated holder, but having the color will boost your mental focus.

Oil: Select the oil that represents your need. In the case of a money spell, Patchouli oil will work better for prosperity.

Herbs and Spices: Just like the oil, your herb should also represent your need. In the case of a money spell, you can go for ground cinnamon, which is associa-

ted with wealth; Dragon's blood, which increases the power of spells; and ground ginger, which hasten results.

Learning to Choose Correspondence

Correspondences are like keywords in any work-projects, books, etc. They are highlighters of your intention and your need. When you lose your focus on these, you are sure to get your results as fast as possible. When you are learning Wicca, you need to make these correspondences your friends. Check the internal insatiably for these correspondences.

You will find a useful table with the most popular correspondences there for you. This is an accumulation of several ones found on the internet. In other words, it will serve as your thesaurus.

Before you get to the table, however, you must make a quick assessment of the reasons for choosing any correspondence like what word can you associate with what you desire? It is not compulsorily a specific correspondence, but upon taking a closer look at some colors, you will find yourself enjoying certain benefits as a result of what you attach to these colors. In the case of money, green can remind some people about money, while to others red, brown, or gold can be the pointer to wealth for them.

In other words, you don't necessarily need to have certain ones before your wish is fulfilled.

Red

Assertiveness, courage, creativity, energy, passionate, love, sex

Orange

Ambition, concentration, eloquence, legal issues, intellectual pursuits, success

Yellow

Attractiveness, clarity, happiness, intelligence, persuasiveness, travel.

Green

Growth, fertility, harmony, health, prosperity, wealth

Blue

Dreamwork, healing, intuition, loyalty, peace, spirituality

Purple

Beauty, compassion, feminity, partnerships, romantic/innocent love

White

It can serve any purpose and can be interchanged

with any missing color. Cleansing, purification, truth, reflecting energy.

Black

Absorbing energy, banishing, breaking bad things like bad habits or hexes, etc., discovering hidden wisdom, protection, self-defense

Brown

Abundance, family, friends, gardening, grounding, pets, stability

STEP 4: DRESS THE CANDLE

This part plays a major role in the act of candle magic. For your magic to really become functional, you would need to have a secure connection between you and your goal. And for that to happen, the candle will serve as the psychic link between you and your torch. Thus, we can say that dressing the candle is the act of preparing your candle to develop the needed psychic link between you and your desired goal. Now, for this to come to reality, do these and you are good to go.

20 ## Oiling of Candle

Regardless of the type of oil you have chosen, the first

process is that you rub your candle with the selected oil. To do that is so simple; as you will only drop oil on your palm and then use it to, rub the oil.

Now when we are dealing with rubbing oil, different people have created different methods to ensure it gives the desired result.

Rubbing of the candle from the top and going all the way down.

Rubbing the candle from the bottom and going all the way to the top.

Rubbing the candle from the bottom to attract something to yourself but if you rub it downward, you're doing so to send something away.

Rubbing from the upward or downward from the center is another way to go about it.

Rubbing from the bottom and moving to the top to rob the oil but stop at the center. Then, you rub from the center to the bottom

Visualizing Your Intent

Regardless of the method, you favor in the rubbing of your candle, if your mental state is shaky, it will affect your work. To have the desired result, it is advisable that you keep visualizing what you wish to see at the end of the day. This requires that your energy is duly

poured into the candle. One way to ensure you are focused on your visualization is for you to chant as you rub. As you rub and chant at the same time, your energy level will increase. To know that your energy level is building, you might feel a tingly feeling on your hand, or you discover that your candle is pulsing with energy.

Keeping at It Until You Get a Fully Charged Candle
The process is such that you have to continue regardless of the number of time you have done it until you get the desired result. You need to feel the pulse on your hand. And to get this impressive result, you might need to rub it for about 50 to 100 times. Don't stop at it until you are assured that it is fully charged.
To keep the candle charged can be done at any time. You don't necessarily have to do at the same time as you want to cast the spell.

Charging Your Herbs and Spice

If you vividly remember, these are just aids, they will help in the correlation of the energy around you. To use them, you only need to charge them before-hand. To do this, roll the charged candle around them. You might decide to sprinkle them with the candles. No matter the method employed, you must keep your vision in check.

Using Runes and Symbols Also

Another optional energy supplement you can ensure a heightened level of energy is to inscribe runes or symbols on the candles. You can decide to scratch anything you want on the wax of these candles. It doesn't matter what you use as long as it helps you.

Preferably, choose something that will really connect you to candle. That way, you can easily make the change you want.

STEP 5: CAST YOUR SPELL AND LI-GHT THE CANDLE

This is a crucial part. Casting of spell and lighting the candle requires that firstly have your seats in front of your candle.

Meditation

This is a really important aspect that would hasten your relaxation process. To really get it, you could easily breathe slowly. All you will do here is to help you release your tension and free the intrusive thoughts, fears, and worries. One way you can quickly release the tension in your body is by imagining that your tensed thought are some balloons you're releasing.

Visualization

Another way to do this is by visualizing your goal and seeing yourself enjoying the fruit of the labor.

Think of the Feeling

The next thing you need to do is to work until you can easily feel the same type of joy you will get when you have gotten the result of your desire. If at the end of your goal, you will feel relaxed, then you need to work on that.

Explore your feelings when you eventually have a new look. Having this feeling will charge you and help you prepare for the next time.

Visualizing

Hold on the imagination and run on it. Repeatedly use it as you chant. This will increase your level of energy and would help you in getting the feeling needed at that point. You will get a new burst of energy in you. As soon as you get the feeling of energy bursting through you, light the candle.

Connecting to the Candle

The next step would be for you to focus your imagination on the light aura you can see outside the flame. At this point, imagine it grow and become bigger per time. Then, feel it overwhelming the room. Its expansion suddenly outshoots the house and encompasses the universe to get your goal. At this point, you will need to keep at your chanting.

Holding-on to the Visual

The next step is for you actually to see yourself collecting the thing you need. The inclusion of this to the already energized imagination will spur you to get your result.

Step 6: Burning Out and Burying

After you have done the visualization, you should go on to allow it to burn. Don't worry if it goes out before it burns out. However, as soon as it is done, the next step is to bury it. Even if it has been burnt to ashes, you need to bury it.

STEP 7: CLEANSING YOUR CANDLE

If you understand the true meaning of cleansing now, you would not need any significant introduction for each for them. On a closer look, the word cleansing is actually cleansing but on a different level. A regular cleansing would have been on a physical level, but this time, we are looking at a spiritual level. The focus here is cleansing the source of energy.

To look at it from another angle is to suggest that one is trying to detach oneself from previous vibrations. It's like the regular need for cleansing in our lives. Take that you have moved from one place to another and have attracted dust, you would definitely need a form of cleansing or the other. That can be said of the spiritual level. Before allowing another set of energy pass

through your body or the things you want to use, it is right for you to cleanse it.

Let's check out the general methods you can employ before we laser our focus on cleansing candles:

1.   Running the object through a burning incense specially prepared for cleansing.

2.   Burying the object on the earth until you are ready to use it. Not only that, but you can also bury in other cleansing object s that have the same power the earth can provide such as salt, dirt, or even cornmeal.

3.   Using salt for its cleansing by sprinkling or spraying the object with salt. Well, as suggested above, you can also bury the object in salt. Remember that the object has a higher tendency of rust when placed in a salt solution overnight. You just have to use your discretion about it.

4.   Place it under running water.

5.   You might also decide to use the fire solution by waving the object fire or a candle. If what you want to cleanse is a pouch of herbs, you don't want to place it near the fire.

6.   Use besom, also referred to as blessed broom, for sweeping away negativity.

Back to the cleansing of the candle. Unlike the numerous methods written up there, you might need to go over-cleansing your candle in a totally different way. Some of them have the same features as the regular ways prescribed.

26

These four ways are the most preferred of all in cleansing your candle.

1.   The Sage Fire

This method is simply you holding the candle atop an incense or sage smoke.

2.   The Moonlight Bath

Another preferred method is to leave your candle out for it to be bath by the moon over the night.

3.   The Salt Grave

As prescribed earlier, the salt solution is one of the top methods of cleansing any object. However, in the case of the candle, you will need to bury it for a whole day. This will make the process effectively.

4.   Alcohol Bath

Another method you can use is to use alcohol to cleansing by rubbing it from the bottom to the top. In a case the candle is such that it is in a glass, then you will need to rub the alcohol on any exposed areas as well as on the glass.

Remember that the most crucial aspect of your cleansing is you focusing on your goal as you carry out the ritual.

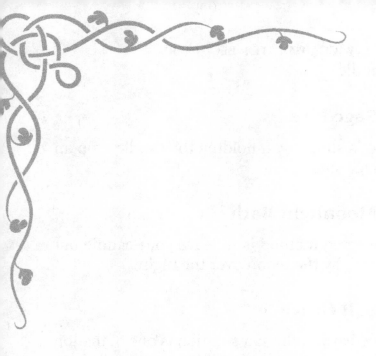

28

CHAPTER - 3
Herbs

The definition you get from a Botanist might be totally different from any other, but for a Wiccan, the most proper description would be to call herbs any plant beneficial for humans. This might actually include when they are used for cooking, as medicine, for fragrance or any other functional function. The implication, therefore, is that they are not limited to only plants but are also found among trees, shrubs, fruits, flowers, grasses, and any other plants classified among 'weed.'

As a Wiccan, herbs are not only seen as one when they are beneficial to humans, but they are also seen as part of herbs when they are toxics. Some good examples are belladonna and henbane, which are both deadly.

When you become deeply immersed in the knowledge of herbs, you will realize that there is actually no difference in the healthiness of herbs but the way they are being used. However, if you are just starting out, it is wise to go with the rules set out for these types of thin-

gs. Heed the traditions that have been set for it.
In fact, if you will be casting a spell that involves toxic spells and recipes, opt for safer herbs.

THE FORMS YOU CAN USE HERBS

The usage of herbs is in three different ways. We have the fresh, dried, or those used as an essential oil.

Fresh Herbs

To get fresh herbs, you can go in two ways. One of them is to grow your own herbs. This affords you all the fresh herbs you need. You might eventually dry the excess or even kept for future use. To grow herbs, you don't need to go on a serial journey of getting a large expanse of land. You can choose your balcony or windowsill as the point of growing your herbs. Sometimes, you don't have to worry about increasing different herbs as some herbs accommodate other herbs, for example, you can grow rosemary and lavender together.

The other way you can get fresh herbs is by getting them from other people. All you need to do is to arm yourself with the right knowledge on how to go about it. Try reading books or taking a course to help you know the type of herbs to get. When you are sure of the ones you will be getting, you can get them from your neighbors. Ensure you make a proper request from the owner before getting. More so, avoid stripping an area totally of herbs because you would want others to benefit from its usefulness.

Dried Herbs

When you need to make spells, tea, or take your bathe, you can turn to the dried herbs. To get them is simple. Dry fresh herbs and you have them ready when you require them. Drying it, however, requires a bit of work from you. Tie the fresh herbs into bunches and then hang them upside, ensuring they can be easily circulated by air.

In case you are not adept at growing your herbs, you can get them at any shops. In fact, you have a higher chance of getting your choice when you order them online.

USING HERBS FOR MAGIC

Bathing: Herbs are useful for a ritual healing bath. When you are about to have this, get a sachet. If you don't have access to one, try using a hessian bad and tie it up with a string. Pour fresh herbs and use it for ritual healing baht.

Oils: As pointed out before, you can get oil from herbs. You can make them yourself. To do that, place the herb in the oil you wish to use, allow it to steep for a few days and there you have your herbed oil.

Incense: Burning herbs for their scents is another way to go about its usefulness. A lot of people have used

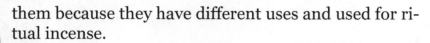

them because they have different uses and used for ritual incense.

Teas

Herbs are not limited to oiling and bathing alone, you can also use them for tea. If you want those made already, you only need to get them at a shop but if you want the fresh one, simply seep it in hot water.

Charms and Sachets

To get this result, pour the herbs into a small bag and direct its usage towards your desire.

Spells

Well, as seen before they are useful for various spells.

COMMONLY USED HERBS IN MAGIC

Find below some of the most popular herbs used for magic.

Bay leaves

Planet: Sun
Element: Fire
Gender: Masculine

32

- To protect against and avoid being hexed or jinxed. If you scatter and sweep them up, you are

creating a protective boundary for yourself.
• When placed under the pillow, it induces prophetic dreams.

Echinacea

Planet: Mars
Element: Earth
Gender: Masculine
• It can help you to strengthen your powers.
• It also gives emotional stamina during difficult times.
• When placed in a vase in the house, it encourages prosperity for the household
• When included in a spell or charm, it increases effectiveness.

Mint

Planet: Venus
Element: Water
Gender: Female
• For the promotion of energy, communication, and vitality.
• For relieving headaches. You only need to inhale the steam from the leaves placed in boiling water.
• Useful for inviting happiness and good fortune into the home. You just have to make it into a floor wash.

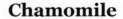

Chamomile

Planet: Sun
Element: Water
Gender: Masculine

- Used to get lucky and attract love.
- Useful for prosperity wishes and for the attraction of money.
- When served tea, it helps in relaxing.
- When used as an incense, it serves as a mean aid for sleep or meditation.
- When added to a bath or used to wash your face and hair, it helps in attracting love.
- As a bath for children, it protects them for evil in people's hearts.

Lavender

Planet- Mercury
Element- Air
Gender- Masculine

- To facilitate sleep, peace, love, and purification.
- To aid relaxation and enable open-mindedness during meditation.
- For the sleep pillows and bath spells.
- If you want love in your life, all you need to do is to hang in your house or even carry a few sachets about.

Rosemary

Planet: Sun

Element: Fire
Gender: Masculine

- It had traditionally served as a memory spells.
- Known for its ability to keep witches out.
- Useful as love and lust incenses or even potions.
- When drunk as a tea, it keeps the heart at alert.

HOW TO CHARGE AND CLEANSE HERBS AND PLANTS

The process of charging and cleansing herbs is simple and should not be avoided for any reason. When you are using herbs, you need to always charge them before even taking them off the ground. When you eventually pull them off the ground, you also need to cleanse.

For a fresh plant especially, the best thing to do is to charge the herbs when you plant them or when you are about to use them for a magical purpose. This goes for those you take from other sources.

CHARGING YOUR HERB

Use the Floor

You can either sit on the ground outside or within the house. Any way you decide to go, the next step would be to rid yourself of any disturbing thoughts and then focus on yourself. Use your mind to grab the energy around you and create a connection between your own energy and that of the earth beneath you.

Be Full to the Brim

When connected to the earth source, feel yourself being filled to the top by the power of the divine. This will give you access to redirect the energy somewhere else.

Transmission

Now that you have the power coursing through your vein, the next step will be to seek out the herbs and redirect the power of the divine on it. To do this, stare at the energy or be in contact with it. Then, cast spell on it.

Then say:

Plants of life and all that's living With the magic that is ever giving With every minute that you grow Our energies, combined, will flow Increasing your potency with every hour I fill you with my Magical Power As I share with you this energy Charged you are, So Mote It Be!

This same process would help when you aim to cleanse it. However, this time, all that is required of you is to remove every negativity from it and redirect positive energy into it.

CHAPTER - 4
Crystal

Crystals are stones that are filled with wonders. They are full of information that will eat deep into the time meant for any other thing because of the type of wonder they evoke. They have a way of communicating about the infinite, about life in the earth. Various lords and ladies have revered it because of the power it holds. Even talismans take high esteem in it.

In the present word, Wicca has turned to it for healing, enhancing energy, and numerous other magical reasons.

THE MAGIC OF CRYSTAL

Energy Manipulation

This type of magic is such that would demand a whole deal of information from you and would indeed be necessary. The elemental magic you will need to learn

how to practice with the crystal is how to sense, raise, or project it.

As a beginner, you might find it hard to become attuned to its knowledge, but upon frequent exercises, you will definitely get the expected result. As with any new thing, you need to follow the due procedure until you are assured of your ability to use methods that suit you.

CLEAR QUARTZ CRYSTALS

This exercise will be done with the aid of numerous clear quartz crystals. One good thing is that almost all the crystals available have the natural tendencies to defend against evil and can also be used to attract prosperity. Like an empty vase, they don't hold any particular power of their own. In other words, they have the neutral ability and can only amplify any energy projected upon them or brought near the.

As stated before, they work as a vase in the sense that they are either projective or receptive. Well, like every crystal, Quartz crystals also work as a vase. You cannot associate any form of energy with them because of their uniqueness but you can easily use them to store energy or transmit energy from one place to another. They are only amplified when they are near a form of energy or when they are projected upon.

To use it, therefore, you will need to do certain things.

Cleaning the crystal before use
It is best when you cleanse it before time by soaking
in salt water overnight. You can also smudge or have
them buried in the earth during moon cycles. This will
help them get rid of any previous association with any
energy.

Gather Them

You need to place in a sort of container that has several
compartments. If you don't have such a compartmen-
tal container, then you need to opt for containers for
each of them. You also need to ensure these containers
are identical so you will not be able to differentiate
them from one another.

STAGE ONE
INCREASING THE ENERGY

The steps of this first stage are very simple.

Meditate

You need to enter a meditative state as this will help
you get relaxed for the next steps.

Pick An Emotion

Now, you need to ensure you are focused on a natural
feeling, especially one you can easily remember at that

moment and one that you can easily hold on to. It can be joy or sadness or trepidation or desire or peace. Regardless of the type, all you need is to pick one that will help you stir up your desire. Simply focus on the ones that have held you bound that day as this will help you increase and maintain the energy level

Now that you have chosen the energy to allow yourself to grow into the height of the emotion. Allow the feeling increase and don't try to put a stop on it. Let the frenzy continue. At this point, you might want to utilize chanting or rocking or dancing. Use whatever you can to help you unearth this energy from the part it has been hidden.

Solidify This Energy

Your emotional energy would need a sort of thing to make it real. So, you might want to make it less abstract by giving it something to be identified by. You might want to use colors or the reaction you expect them to have. You might want to associate it with a certain style of things. When you have done this, you have prepared yourself for the second part of the energy.

STAGE TWO
PROJECT YOUR ENERGY

This next step will require more action than the first, and you should be prepared for that as well.

Raise the Emotion of the Crystal

One more beautiful thing that can actually explain the
beauty of things for you is the way you will be found
projecting your energy to other things.
Pick one of the crystals and raised the emotion of this
crystal. Then, visualize this emotion.

Pour Your Emotion

When you have imagined the emotion represented as
color or something substantial enough, you will then
need to see yourself pouring your feelings into any of
these crystals. When you're done, with pouring your
emotion on one of the crystals, you will need to label
with anything that will make it outstanding. You might
even tie a tag to the crystal. Then, return it.

Repeat the Pouring Exercise

This time, you might need to raise a different emotion
for a different crystal. Ensure your previous emotion is
poured only one the same crystal as this will ruin the
original plan. Always aim for one emotion per crystal.

STAGE THREE
SENSE THE ENERGY

The next step is to sense the energy poured into each
of these crystals. The aim is to enable you to have the
same power that has been poured into the crystals

when the time is nigh. To do this:

Remove The Tags And Blindfolds

The essence of this is to help you avoid the bags or containers or the energy attached to them. So, to do this, you will need to remove any tag or anything that will help you easily identify them. Then, you should blindfold yourself so as not to see the crystal beforehand. With that done, you won't be deceiving yourself by having the intended emotion just by seeing the name. Now that you are blindfolded, scatter the arrangement of the bags randomly until you are sure you can't keep track of their emotions anymore.

Meditate into Neutrality

You need to meditate and have yourself revert to a receptive state. This will help the next steps.

Sense Them

Now, you don't have to open the containers to know what you are doing. All that is required of you is to see the next energy with your body. How do you do this? Simple! Open the container and place your hand over the bag. You are to touch the crystal. Here, you are only trying to sense the emotions poured into each crystals. Sense the energy radiating from the crystal until you are sure. Now, you can take a peek at it. If you are not sure, don't beat yourself up. It's typical for beginners. Simply go to the next step and try to work around it.

Then repeat these stages until you are sure you are ready to go.

Keep Practising

To do more works, you will need to keep practicing by
ensuring you can sense the energy of a crystal. To have
a quick success at this, have crystals around and try to
sense their energies per time.

Pick a part of the body for each of the emotions. With
time, this emotion will give that part of the body a feeling that will help you understand when you have en-
countered such energy. Also, you can carry a particular
crystal with you. As much as you can, avoid taking the
negative emotions with you.

If you genuinely need to understand the power of these
negative energies, you should allow them to be around
you when you are at home and alone. Even when it is
done, have a thorough cleansing afterwards. You can
also cleanse the energy of these crystals to give them
the chance to be used for other positive things.

Don't forget the container as well.

ESSENTIALS CRYSTALS FOR BEGIN-
NER WICCANS

Many people have spread outrageous claims about the
number of crystals a good witch should have. There
is no amount of crystal, whether zero or a thousand

would automatically give the status a good witch. The only thing that matters is your desire to either expand your training. Some people do not find fun in the numerous processes involved in using crystals; thus, they focus on other aspects. And to some others, this is the best thing to happen to this world, which makes them have hundreds and hundreds of works. You are the architect of your craft and should be the only determinant of its progress.

This list comprises of about five essentials ones that will help you even if you have an idea of Wicca.

CLEAR QUARTZ

This the second most prevalent mineral ever extracted from the Earth's crust and can be extracted on every planet. Being universal, it has the potential of being sold at a cheaper rate.

Its name was derived from the Greek word 'Krustallos, which means 'ice' because of the assumption that it was a kind of ice formed by the gods. And for a long while, dating back to the Middle Ages, this crystal has been useful in the prediction of the future.

Till date, any lover of crystals would have a piece of clear quartz, probably because it also serves as crystals. It has the chance of coming in various types and can also be referred to as pure quartz, seeing that it is transparent had lacked a particular. A lot of crystals are actually classified under this category too.

Uses of Clear Quartz

EASY REPLACEMENT OF OTHER CRYSTALS

Clear quartz serves as a replacement for almost any other crystals. Some modern scientists have placed it as one with the power of sending, receiving, and storing energy both on the physical and metaphysical levels.

Protection and Healing

Also, it can amplify things and have been used for protecting oneself from wiles of the enemies and hasten the healing process

Sharpens Focus

Quartz also can help you focus when you seem to find it hard to do. Regardless of where you need it, the presence can help you out in performing the task at hand mainly if it's centered on studying

Versatile

This crystal is also versatile and can perform the action needed in any spell work or process in such ways as helping out with dream works, meditations, divination, or the healing procedures.

ROSE QUARTZ

This is a variety of quartz because it is a rosy pink hue color. This presence of this color is a result of a little amount of titanium present in its body. Having various shades of the color, its type, it can also be purple or lavender.

It is regarded as one that is filled with unconditional love. Most times, they are carved to form a heart shape, maybe to bring the idea to life. This crystal is mostly found in the possession of witches that have a stronger interest in the issue of love or self-love.

Usage of Rose Quartz

For the Creating Bonds
On different occasions, it has been used in the purification and opening of heart at different levels to help in the promotion of love, friendship or even love.

For Internal Healing

It has also been used towards the inner healing and getting the feelings of peace. Some others have employed it in getting comfort when grieving, going through a heartbreak period or even when anxious.

 ## Protects Internal Feelings

It serves a means of protection against any form of

emotional pollution. Mostly, its focus is on dispelling of negativity. It has the potential for encouraging self-forgiveness and creating acceptance.

To Hasten Mental Illness

As its focus is mainly on treating the inside, you can use it to cure the internal aspect of your body. Despite not serving as a replacement for therapy and medication, it can be used to hasten the healing process.

AMETHYST

Like the others, it is a variant of quartz that has a color formed the iron deposited in it when it was developing. It comes in different shades of purple, which often make it look dark.

When to Use Amethyst

Tranquilizer
It helps in relieving any emotional wreckage or negative emotions like rage, mood swings, anxiety, irritability, etc.

Spiritual Awareness

You can use it to be spiritually aware of things around you. It performs this function by opening your intuition level as well as help in enhancing your psychic

abilities.

Cleansing Powers

It has a power that helps in the healing process and also cleanses the body.

Enhances

It helps in improving things that require focus. Thus, it can be stated that it enhances the memory and brings improvement on your motivation level.

Restraining Power

Another belief is that it can help drunks in remaining sober. This same belief was practiced in the middle age when the Catholic Church used it more often to prevent the priests from remaining sober. There are old fables that point to its ability to help drunks stay sober.

Dreams

Another problem a lot of people have faced is the ability to remember and understand dreams, but with it, you can quickly be relieved of insomnia and can have your spiritual wisdom exposed. With it also, you can prevent nightmares.

48

SELENITE

This crystalline comes from the mineral gypsum family. It has the ability to revert to gypsum when placed
in water. Because of its origin, it can also be transparent and colorless.

Most times, it comes in varieties of color, especially
green, brown and orange.

Uses of Selenite

Enhances Mind
One major work attributed to it is the ability to expand
the awareness of the mind as well as that of one's sur-
roundings. What it does actually is to give your mind
access to guidance from the various spiritual guides lo-
cated in the crown and higher-crown chakras.

Helps with Frequent Problems

As it is with the moon, some problems are such that
leave and return to people. Selenite can stop this problem uniquely when it is placed under the focus of the
moon, seeing that it got its name from the Greek goddess of the moon.

Pregnancy

You can also use it for anyone pregnant or wants a
baby or even those that are raising children.

Timelessness Allowed

With it, you can quickly get pieces of information from the past and those of the future. In other words, witches love its ability to transport their minds to any time needed of it.

Great Meditation Instrument

Another thing it does is to give room for peace and helps in the meditative process. It purges the mind of confusing matter and helps focus after filling the heart with deep contentment.

HEMATITE

Formed from iron oxide, it comes in different dark colors like black, red, brown, or a combination of the different colors. It gets its name from both Greek and later Latin because of its most popular color, reddish-brown.

Usage of Hematite

Grounding and Protection
It can increase the way you connect to the earth and help you exude safety and security.

Internal Strength

50

With it, you can easily get inner strength and even be

filled with undetected courage or endurance.

Helps in Refocusing

Also, it can be used in the enhancing of original thoughts or memories. Often referred to as the 'stone of the mind, it helps in the stimulation of concentration as well as focus.

Good-luck Attractor

It is believed to have the ability to cause good luck. In the ancient Roman, it was believed that anybody smeared with hematite will be invisible in battle. Many people have used different legal situations and have recorded a wide range of success.

Removal of Negativity

When you look at it on another level, you will discover its ability to balance the different nervous systems of the body and enhance the way the energy of the body, as well as that of the body, is focused. Removing negativity, it also helps in the prevention of other's negativity coursing through our body.

OTHER MAJOR CRYSTALS USED IN WITCHCRAFT

There are several other important Crystals you shouldn't overlook.
Celestite
This crystal is believed to have helped astral travelers or those trying it out.

Diamonds

Many believe that diamonds amplifies the properties of any other crystal it encounters.

Galaxite

Also referred to as the "aura stone," it can protect or balance your aura or that of any environment.

Lepidolite

This stone is made of lithium. Many have recommended it for treating those suffering bipolar disorder because of its ability to balance moods or even calm negative emotions.

Meteorites

This crystal is believed to help with the connection to the universe's energy.

Pink manganocalcite
Is also referred to as the "Reiki Stone" due to its fascinating ability to seemingly increase healers' powers.

CLEANSING CRYSTAL

The cleaning processes are on different levels. If you want to cleanse it from physical dirt, all you need to do is to clean it with lukewarm water and if necessary, with a gentle detergent.

Now, cleansing on the metaphysical level is of a different type. More so, you should ensure you do this if the crystal is new or when your crystal has been touched or used by someone else.

Breath Cleansing

You can use your breath on it by gently breathing on it. All you have to do is to ensure you are focused on it, pouring your intention of cleansing into it.

Salt Water Soak

You can also use salt water for its cleansing as long as it doesn't have any crack.

Candles

Another way you can cleanse it is by lighting candles on it. All you have to do is to chants or pray on it while washing it.

CHARGING YOUR CRYSTAL

There are two ways of charging your crystal.

Usage of Light

To do this, you will need natural lights. You can use either sunlight or moonlight. In the case of sunlight, you will soak them there. However, in the case of moonlight, you intend to bath them with radiance.

Shared Energy

Place them amidst potted plants, where they will be absorbing the energies of these plants.

CHAPTER - 5
Tarot

Tarot started out as a rich park of card suitable for games and have been used for such games as the Italian tarocchini, French tarot, etc. Many of these games are still in play today. However, in the late 18th century, these parks of the card began to have a deeper meaning than just the game card. This even became the essence of many witches. When people noticed the rate at which game cards were used to read the future, they decided to create custom cards for this purpose.

Despite this, the patterns of creation are almost the same as the conventional game. The four suits remain as they are by region:

- French suits in Northern Europe
- Latin suits in Southern Europe
- German suits in Central Europe.

Each suit has 14 cards, ten pip cards numbering from

one (or Ace) to ten and four face cards (King, Queen, Knight, and Jack/Knave). More so, the tarot comes with a different 21-card trump suit as well as a single card referred to as the Fool. The fool is such that can move in any direction as the regular suits. These cards are still played like regular cards whenever there is no occult association.

Although some history points to other native countries like Egypt or Indian as the origin of these aspects of Wicca. But the real documentation of its use started in Europe in the late 18th Century.

READING TAROT CARD WITH PLAYING CARDS

There is no need for an exclusive deck of the card before you can perform your magic using tarot. You might indeed have a better handle at it if you truly have the original tarot card. But if you don't have access to it now, learn the methods through a standard deck of cards.

Hearts

It represents cups. These depict emotions, feelings, relationships.

56

Spades

These represent the sword. They represent thinking and communication.

Diamonds

They represent pentacles, coins, or discs. They show practicalities, material world

Clubs

They stand for wands, rods, batons, or staves. They represent creativity or action

Now that you understand the summarized ways of looking at it, you can easily decipher their meaning.

Hearts

Like cups, they hold information about emotions and feelings. They are not limited to love but deal with the various other emotions available in the history of man. In most cases, the hearts symbolize relationships, which serves as the home of numerous other emotions.

Spades

There are like swords and connected to our level of thoughts and the way we communicate with others. They are all about logicality. Thus, you can include

lying under the state. It has focused on studying and making decisions. Like the swords, you can see either constructive or destructive actions. Some of these actions are the way we do things forcefully, or the assertion of power, the display of ambition, the exhibition of courage, or dealing with conflict.

Diamonds

They represent pentacles, coin, or disc. They are the reflection of everything practical or those that relate to the material stuff available. They are all about real things and those things that affect the body like health issues.

Clubs

They symbolize wands, rods, batons, or staves. They deal with actions like creativity, business transactions, relationship issues, etc. Also, they are about adventure, risk-taking as well as competition

MEANING OF THE NUMBERS OF TAROT CARDS

 Having an excellent knowledge of how the numbers work will give a solid background to card reading. Every aspect of the card can either be a positive or

58

negative result. For example, eight means movement while the negative side meaning stagnation or lack of movement.

TAROTS CARDS AND THEIR MEANING

Cards Numbers	Positive Meanings	Negative Meaning
Ace	They always positive. They represent newness	None.
Two	Balance	Delay or waiting
Three	Connection	Division, mixed-up communication, or plans gone awry.
Four	Stability	Feeling stuck
Five	Disturbance	Challenges that can lead to expansion.
Six	Harmony	The lack of or yearning for it, but sixes are rarely negative
Seven	Mystery	Being overly concerned with superficialities
Eight	Movement	Lack of movement, stagnation
Nine	Growth	Satiety
Ten	Completion	New beginnings, or new endings

Remember the suits correspondence up there. You will now have to connect the two together. This table will help in the creation of that.

Ace

Hearts: New friendship, romance
Spades: New insights, realizations
Diamonds: New project, job, win or , home
New idea, business, action.

Two

Hearts: Deepening attraction
Spades: Failure to communicate
Diamonds: Waiting on results
Planning and preparation.

Three

Hearts: Joy in company, friendship, celebration
Spades: Miscommunication, misunderstanding
Diamonds: Teamwork, improvising skills.
Leadership, exploration

Four

Hearts: Turning inwards, apathy,
Spades: Recuperation, recovery, contemplation
Diamonds: Miserliness, possessiveness
A goal achieved, rest from action

Five

Hearts: Loss, despair
Spades: Discord, dishonor, hollow victory

Diamonds: Loss of possession or job or money
Competition, disagreement, irritation

Six

Hearts: Childhood, nostalgia, good memories, an old friendship resumes

Spades: Moving on, travel, mentally getting to a better place

Diamonds: Giving or receiving money, a pay-rise, obtaining resources

Victory, achievement, passing exams.

Seven

Hearts: Daydreaming, wishful thinking, choices

Spades: Lying, deceitfulness, theft, irresponsibility

Diamonds: Reassessment, turning point, mild dissatisfaction

Defense, conviction, strong belief.

Eight

Hearts: Emotional detachment, leaving love behind, making a hard choice

Spades: The illusion of being trapped, powerlessness

Diamonds: Being finicky, focus, practice
The organization, moving, quickly, pregnancy.

Nine

Hearts: Satisfaction, sensual pleasure, spiritual growth

Spades: Nightmares, problems, worry, guilt

Diamonds: Independence, self-reliance, increasing wealth

Continuing a battle, endurance, physical strength.

Ten

Hearts: Contentment, fulfillment, joy, family

Spades: Giving up, victimization, martyrdom

Diamonds: Great wealth, family property, inheritance

Carrying burdens, responsibility, and debt.

YOU CAN READ THE NEXT SETS OF CARDS IN DIFFERENT WAYS. YOU CAN READ IT AS EITHER A PERSONALITY TRAIT OR THINGS ABOUT REAL PEOPLE

Jack/Knave

Hearts: Falls in love easily, romantic, chatterbox

Spades: Rebel, fights for a cause, intellectual, political

Diamonds: Reliable, hard-working, quiet, hidden depth

62

Unreliable, hotheaded, risk-taker, athletic

Queen

Hearts: Emotional, dependent, empathic

Spades: Sharp, intelligent, ruthless, insightful, organized

Diamonds: Practical, warm, dependable, motherhood

Energetic, career-minded, untidy, disorganized.

King

Hearts: Wise, tolerant, diplomatic, feeling, patient

Spades: Introspective, ethical, communicator, stern

Diamonds: Self-made, business owner encouraging enjoys the fruits of his labors, jolly

Creative, forceful, entrepreneurial charismatic, hot-tempered.

HOW ACCURATE ARE TAROT CARD READING

There is something about Tarot card reading you should remember whenever you read it: they are never wrong. However, the accuracy of its interpretation is totally dependent on the person delivering the messa-

ge. Before you consider the usage of cards, you should consider the following factors.

The Question Asked

When you ask your questions, you need to ensure it is accurate. A lot of people like to ask questions based on wishful thinking instead of the things they have happening around them. Take a good example of a woman that met a man on a business trip. Their meeting caused them to fix a date.

This woman really enjoyed herself on this date and was soon swooning in the joy of the future. To her, they shared more than chats about their work. She believed the chemistry building up between them was worth the risk of knowing how things will pan out.

When she visited a tarot reader, her question was focused on the future than the right issue. Her question, like those of many tarot readers, are rigged with emotional demand. At this point, the interpreter might have to struggle with the response of the card drawn. Thus, the necessity to interpret the best way they can. To have the right question, you must ensure their accuracy and honesty.

Tarot Card Can't Reveal the Future

64

To read tarot cards means that you are prepared for the synergy of all the energies, emotions, situations, and influences as well as events happening at that exact time. When you also add that synchronization of the energies between the client and the reader, you will realize that the influence will be accurate in its score. This has shown itself to be the reason you can never get the same result from any two people.

This alone has influenced the reason no reader can shape the future. The future is utterly unknowable. Anyone can make a prediction only for it to be affected by a new decision or the unexpected change of habit. Therefore, the accuracy of the prediction will suddenly be altered.

If you become a reader as you have simply learned from the top, you should let it be known to your client that the outcome is always never permanent. Because of how temporary they are, you will not find it wise to predict the future for them.

The Present Holds the Best Value

Most clients make the wrong assumption that reading is anything other than the present, and that has always been the reason for the wanton desire for the prediction about the future. Regardless of their hope and aspiration, you should keep reminding them that any prediction they get will be more present-focused than any other time.

Cards Answers Need and Not Want

There have been several cases of people having the

desire to know something else, but the cards bring another answer into view. As a reader, be dauntless regardless of the solution you get because the reading is up to what the cards believe is the right answer for the asked question.

A lot of people have had to go through the ordeal of repeating cards to meet their demands, but they kept meeting a new desire. Some people might even want to know about their own situation only for them to be greeted by an answer relating to other people in their lives. Most times, the card has a way of understanding your innermost desires and worries. When you begin to encounter such a problem, simply explain your situation to the client. If they feel comfortable with your first result, proceed to ask a further question about the answers given.

Try to prepare yourself for any outcome. Possibilities abound, and the cards have a way of picking the right choice.

Readers Have Different Abilities

Of the three types of tarot readers available, the first kind is the most craved for. And these are those readers with psychic abilities. These readers have, over the years, developed their psychic abilities. They only need the card as a springboard for their insights. Their abilities provide them with the chance of getting personal details without a need to ask too many questions. On the other hand, the second group is those trained in the method of the traditions. They have learnt most of the traditional meanings of the cards. In that light, they might not necessarily have the wrong answers to the question but might only have rigid ones. Their interpretation is always brought as it has been poured into them at the inception of their education. They have little ability in interpreting the details of any card. What this set fails to understand is that each card is blessed with its own story. Thus, if they take the cards in a group, they might miss out on the original story being told. On most occasions, they stop the art because they are not building any connection to tarot reading.

The third group, however, are those that mix the meanings of cards with their own intuition. They use their years of experience as well as their memories in determining the answer to their question. In fact, while reading a card, their mind will be buzzed by something entirely random, which coerce them to look at the combination from a different meaning. That way, they seek out hidden meanings to the combinations. This doesn't place them as right, but they definitely find fun in it and are ready to work harder than the second group. So before you help read any card, you should make your client have a knowledge of the type of reader you are. This will help them understand how you intend to interpret what you see. When you let them know you cannot connect to dead relatives or do not have special abilities of the psychic, they will find it easy to take whatever you read.

Tarot Readers Are Humans

In many cases, the readers always try to avoid being on one side of the interpretation. But some others employ it as a means to counsel others. There is every likelihood that a reader would infuse their own worldview into the reading. Things you have experienced that serve as your viewpoints and the memories you have had will definitely creep into whatever you are reading. As much as it is helpful, this can tilt the reading towards the reader than the asking client.

The Tarot Deck Creators Are Also Humans

As stated before, every tarot deck is created by someone. In most cases, the creative process is carried by two or more people. The creators are not only people involved. We still have such people as publishers, printers, and investors. Every one of these people has a certain influence on the eventual creative plan. More so, we also have writers and artists.

Not only those ones. Even the idea each symbolism and correspondence was done by one or other people. Also, if you are to go by the traditional interpretations, they have been altered and modified severally. Different interpretations have gotten updated by new interpretations. And the thing seems to lose more are the views.

You have the right to choose a deck closer to the source like the reproduction of one of the 15th-century decks. Yet, never forget that these decks were initially desi-

68

gned for that play parlor games, and were not intended for fortune-telling or counseling a client on things that bother them.

One other important information is that the origin of tarot was Chinese traditional playing cards. Nonetheless, many tarotists argue that will tell you it was the reverse was the case. Many of them agree playing cards came to Europe through Egypt around 1350. These details, lost overtime, have always been the cause of the differences in these cards.

Even at that, someone seems to find great joy in the creating of some interesting characters to the playing cards to make it an amusing game. Thus, Tarot is not some mystical system channeled by some long-dead psychic from the gods themselves. The cards are simply human inventions.

And we can categorically say that many of the decks in use today are modern. The Rider-Waite, first published in 1907, became a reality as a result of Edward Waite's interpretation of the principles regarding the different branches of esoteric schools of thought as well as the various societies he used to be a member. This particular deck and the Thoth Tarot, which was a creation of fellow occultist, Aleister Crowley, played a major role in the tarots around the world.

All these are to point out that tarots are biased and tilted towards the creator's beliefs. So, make a wise selection of your preferred system and have a thorough understanding of your deck. And it is advisable to

have an in-depth knowledge of the primary deck, one of which had been explained above. This knowledge will help you when you are stuck.

Can All The Cards Have Right Answer?

As much as it cannot be proved, these thought is something that always plays out every now and then. Since the cards only printed images, you might, like many of the clients, assume there must be the answer for the client there. The cards are random and do not hold all the answers. They are connected to all the other cards. This thought alone is one thing that will forever question the objectivity of tarot cards. This question will forever make it hard to fully enjoy or get a more profound meaning from the cards or for the client to fully accept the answer/

To some extent, every aspect of life has been included in one form or another in the cards. This covers such things as disaster, triumph, love lost and found; children, art, work, and illness, death, destruction, and addiction. They have been created with the intention of touching every question of life.

This, therefore, explains why any random card would hold the relevant answers. Consequently, the problem can only come from the reader, whose job is to ensure the right application of that message and interpret the meaning in line with the client's situation. This reader is then encumbered with the burden of teasing out a significant thread of the story in such a way that the client understands the story.

70

It is true that the cards are random, especially after random shuffling and cutting, but you have to agree that they all set to answer the asked question correctly.

What About the Difference between Upright and Reversed Cards?

Some believe a reversed card can have a different meaning than it would when facing upright. It's not a different meaning necessarily; it's where the message falls on the scale of negative to positive. A reversed card will almost always, though not exclusively, point to the negative scale.

An experienced reader understands this principle and will incorporate that positive to negative scale, which is why you will often find many readers only using upright cards.

There's no need to use reversed cards because the imagery is right there. The reversed Eight of Swords shows the positive outlook of the woman freeing herself from her self-imposed prison. All that is needed is the understanding that both ways of reading cards are valid. Thus, when you receive an accurate reading, it is all dependent on the factors as mentioned earlier as well as the tarot reader's process or experience. So, determine which method feels best for yourself and use that one. Following your intuition is an integral part of tarot.

TOP 5 TAROTS CARD DECKS FOR BEGINNERS

As it is with any system, there would surely be some complicated types of tools for making some understanding of the craft. The following tarot card decks are suitable for any beginning Wiccan.

The Akashich Tarot

This tarot is right for you, regardless of the time spent as a witch. When you follow any Tarot guidebook, you will notice that they are the same. However, you must remember that tarot cards are to be interpreted with your intuition, alongside your knowledge and experience.

The creator of this deck ensured they were replaced with cards that are now slightly more positive, yet still realistic. This is similar to the way Doreen Virtue does her decks. This card is great for you when you want to use something more uplifting, but that still makes sense and provides practical everyday advice.

If you feel drawn to Archangels, you will find them in this deck. In case you are not acquainted with the name 'Akashic Records,' note that they are a field of energy, containing every information about human incantation garnered throughout time. These cards are created with that intent. One delightful aspect of it is the wheel of Life spread. This particular beautiful spread uses eighteen cards. And each of these cards is arranged in a pattern that enlightens you about the numerous lessons you are experiencing when dealing with love, career, finances, etc. Also, it guides into using this information to transform yourself.

Reading with this deck is productive no matter the question or subject matter and helps you leave with clarity about a thing that you needed an answer to or weren't aware of.

The Druid Craft Tarot

The Druid Craft deck of card places a Druid and Wiccan spin on the traditional images and archetypes from the Rider-Waite deck. It comes with a full-length guidebook, which had been well-crafted to describe the symbols found in these cards. As a beginner, you can learn a lot with this card since you are not yet acquainted with the tarot but need guidance in finding your own voice and interpretations with the cards.

Rich with different meanings, this deck of cards comes in numerous colors. Some Wiccans believe they have a little more personality than the Rider-Waite cards. The figures in these have facial expressions worthy of being used to clearly discern as well as add character and meaning to your reading. Unlike the Akashic Tarot, this stays pretty true to the Rider-Waite ordering and names of the Major Arcana and pip (minor) cards. The images and symbols are similar as well, but they seem to have more meaning in the ways they are con-

veyed in this deck than the Rider-Waite.

It, however, has the disadvantage of being quite large and difficult to shuffle. Also, be warned that they feature distinct naked parts on some of the characters of these cards. However, you will find no harm in it if you enjoy working with the tarot of Sexual Magic.

The Steampunk Tarot

As described by one of the authors of the deck, the steampunk tarot is an aesthetic that combines past and future. One description says, "[It is] what the past would look like if the future had happened sooner." If you find that appealing, then there is every chance of you enjoying this deck of cards.

Beginner-friendly, this tarot deck comes with its own comprehensive guidebook that will definitely be useful in helping you understand the meanings of the cards. Like the Druid Craft, it used the archetypes of Rider-Waite as its base, yet it has different representations when it comes to symbolism and images. Moreover, the book has a quote before each card description that relates to the meaning.

One exciting aspect is women who are really packed with exciting features. Also, Steampunk features a lot of women on different pip cards, giving them unique styles and personalities. Some of them have some androgynous looks, providing a new meaning to the cards.

The Sacred Rebels Oracle

You cannot help but love the Sacred Rebels deck created by Alana Fairchild. Its differences are so numerous, ranging from angels to spirit animals and ascended masters. But if you much enjoy spirit animals and things of that nature, you will enjoy it.

This set features messages like "Follow Your Own Rhythm" and "In the World, Not of the World." As you may have guessed, the theme of these cards is going against the grain and living a life that is true to you. The card created to help you not compare your life with those of others. These are for people, who quickly grasp the deeper meanings of everything, who explore a world of meaning, even when they are poor at communicating it. These cards will help get out of your head and into your heart.

Coming with a guidebook, each card is created with a step-by-step healing process that you can follow after reading the meaning. This can be especially useful if you combine your reading abilities with energy healing modalities.

The Rumi Oracle

If you like Rumi, beautiful art, descriptions that make you think, and being playful, these Rumi oracle cards are for you. This deck was also created by Alana Fairchild. So rich with meaning, you might find them a bit overwhelming if you try to look at more than one. It is advisable you pull one at a time and sit in quiet contemplation with it, or use one Rumi card to enhance a tarot reading. However, if you decide to use these cards, they have a message for every occasion and can be of great use if you are open to their loving vibration. This is a deck that you could interpret as a beginner without even consulting the guidebook because you can get so much from the words, colors, and figures on the cards. There are enough symbols in them, which those acquainted with spirituality can understand. However, it is best to order the set that comes with the guidebook so you can enjoy the Rumi quotations and descriptions that go along with each card.

Alana Fairchild decks have profound meanings. They are more than just your standard "focus on the positive," simple messages that you might see in more popular oracle decks. Although having positivity is good, here you are faced with the reality of life and the twist of fate.

CHAPTER - 6
Essential Oils

Essential oils are mostly those extracted from plants. Essential can, therefore, is regarded as the pure, undiluted oil extracts. They have not polluted by additive, and this major feature makes them expensive to use. Other types of oil, including fragrance oil, are mixed with additive.

Any oil that has been used to steep oil is regarded as oil infusion.

HOW OILS USED IN MAGIC

Essential oils are not a central part of any magical spell, but they serve more as supplements than ones that have been made to perform the works of the original spell. A lot of witches employ them in the anointing of their ritual tools or any other thing they use, including the crystals, talisman, and element as well as their own bodies. Useful for creating incense, they are an excellent choice for any candle magic or charm

making you might want to be involved.
Their primary work is to help in the enhancement of whatever you want to do. Regardless of the number of scents in them.

THE MAGICAL ASPECT OF ESSEN-TIAL OIL

Many of the scents gotten different plants and used for the oil are necessary for your ritual or spell work for two significant reasons.

Plant Energies

These oils are soaked in the energies of the plants they are derived from even they are trees, shrubs, or flowers. When they are transformed from these plants to their liquid form, they are filled with the magical energies of these plants.

If you remember that plants are living entities and have been created with their own type of energy and intelligence that will help in the harmonization of things in nature.

Although synthetic fragrance oils have the same smell of the real oils, they are not natural. Indeed, some witches have successfully used oils over the past years, many others find it better to use the natural ones.

The Power of Scents

Another power embedded in the essential oil is its ability to elevate the mind with its scent. Some of these oils are such that make the body respond to different emotions. Some of these oils make the heart warm while many others just make us relaxed. Take the scents of myrrh and cedarwood as good examples. They have the power of awakening different things in us and even put in a new frame of mind.

Sometimes, witches are always in need of being in the right state of mind for any event at all. So, when they see channels for it, they explore it without any remorse. Oil has always opened the ways for them to connect to the right energy and state of mind. This reason, definitely, is why you can hardly detach them from any Wiccan or pagan tradition. When the scent of essential oil touches the nose, it helps the mind to remain focused on things needed to be done, and the mind wouldn't have to wander off to other places, especially to the many mundane stuff of our everyday life.

GETTING ESSENTIAL OIL

Because of its use and quality, the prices are always steeped. Yet, you can start by getting only two or three. When you get them, you can either use them individually or by mixing them. As you progress in your Wiccan journey, you can now get more.

N.B: There is a list of essential oil correspondence in the third book of this series.

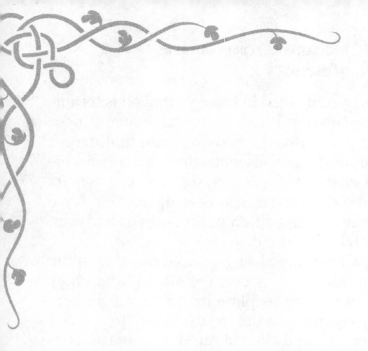

WICCA TOOLS FOR BEGINNERS

CHAPTER - 7
Altar

In numerous religions across the world, there is always a need for a form of the altar or the rest. And this major tool has found its way into the heart of Wicca too. Thus, we can say that the altar is regarded as a sacred space. As a seat of worship, you can place your sacred tools without fear, call on gods and offer things, or even do magic.

Several religions clearly place a sort of demarcation between the altar and the place other activities happen. Only sanctified religious leaders are allowed to use it. The same goes for the Wiccan religion. An altar can be done by individuals; thus, the altar is a sacred place for only the owner. Here, you are not allowed to share it with any form of community. It is your place of private communication to your gods and also a place to celebrate sacred things.

As a Wiccan, the major reason for your altar aside those mentioned above are the ritual celebrations placed for the eight sabbats and the thirteen Esbats, which is the full moon, following the wheel of the year.

HOW A WICCAN ALTAR LOOK

Your altar can be in any form. If you want, you might make your altar permanent in a location you regard as your own. If you consider the site temporary, then you can opt for a movable altar. At this point, you only need to have a flat surface.

A lot of Wiccans will go with the round flat shape of the altar because it helps in the creation of circles. However, if what you have access to is the square or rectangular flat face, you are good to go. The essential things are that one must ensure the altar is made of something natural like wood, metal, or even stones. A lot of people go with wood. But if you cannot afford a new piece of furniture for the sole purpose of creating an altar, then you can easily opt for your coffee table or even any of your household items to the mix. And if you prefer to use location outdoors, you can easily look for a large rock or old tree stump or some other features as an altar.

Don't fuss about it. We will check some ways to go by it.

THINGS TO KNOW BEFORE SETTING UP YOUR ALTAR

As a beginner, setting up your altar is very simple, and you need not worry too much. Before you start the set-up process, you need to attune yourself to these factors

Decoration Has Its Energy

When we get to the aspect of decoration, we can discuss that. But for now, you can always use colored scarves or other fabrics for its decoration. It will help you in the transformation of ordinary furniture into your own altar with fear of any magical implication. In fact, it will give you a sort of magical ambiance needed for the boosting of your energy. A lot of Wiccans prefer to use correspondence of the season as their motive for their decoration.

Take Yule as an example, some might preferably decorate their altar with bright fir leaves as well as holly berries, which they will tie at the different corners of the altar. They might even prefer to scatter flower petals to honor the spring celebration.

Tools Arrangement Have Common Features

The tradition you choose to follow, notwithstanding, does not necessarily determine the way your altar should be. However, some standard features have helped many in doing it right.

One such standard thing is the factor of space. When the space on your table is limited, then you need to understand the tools are more than enough.

Style is Your Choice

You can either make it highly elaborate or simple. The choice is yours. As stated before, you might decide to pattern it after a deity. It is your state.

Use What You Have

Since it is new for some people, they might find it difficult, but after a bit of understanding, you will have no fear. The gods and goddesses are not a bit concerned about the size or shape of your altar.

So, you should understand that it would not be a thing to worry about if your altar cannot be a permanent one. As stated before, you can use anything for your altar. Regardless of what you have, you simply need to utilize what to enjoy it. Like every endeavour, starting small is not to be underestimated. Things evolve on-the-go.

TYPES OF ALTAR

Now that you are fully aware of these factors, you can now worry about the model you want.

Shrine

Here, the core aspect and work to be done is to venerate the gods and goddesses. If you want a place to say prayers, meditate or even honor deities, spirits, household guardians, ancestors, etc. Here, you don't need to worry about it being elaborate. All that you want at this point is to build a place suitable for venerations- a focal point.

84

You can simply place your objects of worship here with a bit of decoration to spice it up. And if you are one that prefers to do sacrifice by incense, this is your grand opportunity. You might want to use some other things to aid you in giving offerings

The few times you might need to employ elaborate decoration will be when you want to have a more massive celebration or seasonal decorations.

Simple, Permanent Shrine

Some people prefer a simple little shrine that deals with what they are doing. These shrines do not need to be elaborate or have any other design than your simple tools to bring it life.

Elaborate Temporary Ancestor's Shrine

You can also create an elaborate but temporary shrine for the Samhain, which is celebrated for both those dead and living. This is set up in a different place for the original shrine.

Box Shrine

This is the type of altar that can be easily packed up when necessary. You might even take it with you, especially when you have people around that.

Ritual Altar

This type of altar requires elaborate decoration because of the full-blown ritual done on it. The best time for its usage is always Esbats, which is the general moon rituals or the Sabbats, which is the holy days of the Wheel of the Year. At this altar, you will find a full ritual set, all laid out on the altar.

This altar is always larger than your permanent shrine since you will be using several tools like athame, wand, cup, pentagram, incense, candles, etc.

Working Altar

When you have a working altar, you are basically using it for doing magic. This is not a shrine. It is here correctly to expose yourself to specific magical energies. As expected, this altar should not be clustered as you need the space for the performance of the energy.

Now, you may begin to wonder if you are not on the wrong for having the desire for more than one altar. There is nothing wrong is having more than two altars. Different people have different altars for different gods and goddesses. Although one altar can perform all the purposes you want to use them for, you can utilize your space.

USE SOME CLASSIC TOOLS TO ADORN YOUR ALTAR

As stated above, some items are worth adding to your tools. Find them below.

Athame

It works as a ceremonial knife or blade and has been favored for different Wiccan and Pagan rituals. Most athames feature black handles. Some of them are inscribed with images, runes, or other symbols. This ceremonial blade is structured towards the channeling of energy or intention, drawing of circles, casting of spells, banishing of negativity, and several other essential magical tasks. If you do not have the athame or cannot afford it at the time of your assemblage, you need not worry. You can use any blade or tool at your disposal. There is no need to purchase a new implement unless you so choose. Other ways you can create Athame on your own are:

Inherited Pocket Knife

To make things better, if you have a pocket knife passed down from a relative, then you have a richer athame, especially if there is meaning or significance attached to it.

A Dull Kitchen Knife

If you have any especially that which has a wooden handle, then you are good to go. You simply need to embellish it with extra fabric and old beads, creating a custom athame for yourself.

A Symbolic Object

In case you do not have any of the above, you can still improvise. Now, if there is a tool you frequently use in your life, work, or art, then you can personalize it as your athame!

Regardless of your craft, your tool can perform magic for you. Let's say you are a writer, choose a pen or pencil. And in the case you are the handy type, pick up any retired wrench and use it. If you are an artist, pick your old paintbrush and customize it as your athame. Whatever tool you choose to use, remember it is your personal altar, and you have the right to personalize, decorate, or embellish it to your liking.

Broom

Brooms, also called besoms, are usually made from a bundle of small twigs tied to a stouter branch, which serves as the broom's handle. In Wicca and other traditions, brooms are used for cleansing or purifying the areas a ritual will be conducted. They are useful for any part of the house.

While these little altar-appropriate, miniature brooms

can be purchased from various makers in specialty stores, they can also be easily constructed by anyone even with little materials. As a beginner, understanding the act of gathering twigs and assembling a personal broom can be a great introduction to the craft; moreover, it is an excellent excuse to walk in the woods.
To start it:

Pick The Twigs

Simply gather a handful or two of twigs from the forest floor and a single, thicker, longer branch to attach them to.

Tie Them

Use thread, twine, or natural material to securely bind the smaller twigs around the bottom of the larger branch. You can research the magical associations of various tree types to inform your selection as you gather materials. Once again, feel free to personalize your creation with any decorations or embellishments that make it your own.

Cauldron

Cauldrons, designed initially to be cooking vessels used over open fires, have been employed both symbolically and practically in Wiccan and pagan practices. They are now functional components of different popular rites and spells and have often been used for the mixing of the different component ingredients used for certain rituals. Various practitioners employ them in the burning of incense, herbs, or dry flowers during moments of meditation.

When it comes to altars, you must remember that your space is always limited. Unless you have the intention of preparing home-cooked meals over an open fire on your altar, avoid getting a big one; instead, opt for something small.

Miniature cast-iron cauldrons can be purchased online or at specialty shops, but any appropriately-sized vessel will do. The alternatives are:

Old tins

If you have an old tin or camping mug that has soaked the energy of the forest from your numerous childhood excursions, then you are good to go.

Part of Creativity

If you have things relating to creativity, then you are good to go. In case you have a piece of ceramic ware you fabricated and kiln-fired in an art class, you are good to go.

Old Vessels

Any vessel can perform the work for you, but you can also get one at a thrift shop. Simply aim for a sort of forgotten container, and you are good to go.

Chalice

The term chalice often conjures images of beautiful-
ly crafted, ornately decorated, oversized goblet fit for
royalty. As it pertains to your altar, a cup is simply a
ceremonial drinking vessel that can perform the same
act as most of the items on this list. It is imbued with
your intentions and used symbolically in a variety of
spiritual tasks.

As a vessel, a chalice can be filled with herbs, ashes,
flowers, and other materials at your discretion, either
for use in a specific spell or ritual or solely for your aesthetic delight. In this way, the vessel is very similar to
the cauldron in both function and appearance. To save
space and money, many practitioners select one vessel
to use symbolically as both a cauldron and a chalice on
their altar.

Incense

Incense is a significant part of any rites. Over the years, it had been used for different purposes in Wiccan
and pagan practices. Moreover, the fragrant smoke
from it has a way of making people favor it. Incense
smoke is frequented by practitioners for the cleansing
circles, altars, and other areas of lingering energy while preparing for a task or ritual. Also, it can be useful in
removing any stale odors emanating from any ill-scen-
ted materials in your craft (e.g., valerian root, gathered

furs or bones, etc.).

Luckily, it favors every budget-conscious pagan with its incredibly low price, while being available everywhere, and having numerous scents. While certain brands are more expensive than others, quality incense can be found at just the right place, including head shops, convenience stores, natural grocers, and online marketplaces like Amazon and eBay.

Pentacle

There is a notion that the Pentacle is a five-pointed star. However, it is merely a talisman that serves a sort of board or drawing magical images or symbols. They tend to be flat and disc-shaped and may be composed of any number of materials. Some pentacles are simply paper or cloth discs, while others may be made from wood or metal. While the five-pointed star or pentagram (inspired by images from the Rider-Waite-Smith tarot deck) is the most commonly used symbol on Wiccan pentacles, any magical logo may be used. Hexagrams, or six-pointed stars, are also popular.

There are various ways of creating your own pentacle at little or no cost. You simply need to
• 	Cut a circular disc out of a spare piece of durable fabric.
• 	Draw your chosen symbol on it with fabric paint.
• 	Alternatively, you could use a soldering iron to burn a symbol into a wooden drink coaster.

Disposable card stock coasters from bars and restaurants can also be painted and repurposed as pentacles. The pentacle is one of the most natural altar tools to make yourself. All you need is your creativity.

Wand

A wand is used by magical practitioners for the casting of spells, directing of energy, and channeling of intention. Among the oldest of the classical altar tools, wands were used by occult practitioners long before the advent of Wicca in the late 19th century. Traditionally, wands have been made of wood, but in practice, they may be composed of any material strong enough to withstand frequent use.

Just like you did the brooms and pentacles, you can create your own wands by using found objects and salvaged materials. One way you can go about is to use a fallen tree. To use a fallen branch, however, like a wand, you would need to:

Durability

You need to be sure about the wood. Ensure it is both hard and tenacious. Brittle woods may break when used, and softwoods are more likely to degrade over time. You may select a branch from a particular plant due to its magical associations or simply use your intuition to choose anyone you feel drawn to. Make sure to choose a branch that has already dried out. Otherwise, its strength and hardness may change over time.

Creating it
Now that you have picked your desired wood, understand that a fallen branch will be best used to connect to the natural world in its unaltered state. You can take it a step further by whittling, carving, and sanding your chosen branch for it appeals to you aesthetically and feels comfortable in your hand.

Personalize it
Whether you shape your new wand or leave it in its natural state, personalize it your own by wrapping the base with your favorite piece of cloth, carving symbols into its surface, or adorning it with stones or jewelry.

Use Other Things
Your wand does not need to be composed of wood. If you are drawn to animals and feel invigorated by nature's endless cycles of life and death, use a scavenged raccoon tibia as your wand. If you love earth's metals or obsess over the countless invisible light waves used by modern technology to transmit information across the world, use an extendable antenna from an old radio.

PERSONALIZE IT WITH OPTIONAL ITEMS

When making your altar, after outfitting it with some of the traditional tools talked about in the previous aspect of this book, you may enjoy personalizing your new space by including some additional elements of your choosing. These additions will out rightly make your altar unique and personal.

You have to pick items that will significantly beautify and align with your goal. Look out for things that resonate with your belief and desire in such a way that you will not worry about spending all the days at your altar. Here are some of the things you can include in your altar.

Minerals, Crystals, and Rocks

Like several others, you can decide to go with any of these, which many practitioners have been known to place on their altars. Crystals' exquisite natural forms, alongside their colors, highlight the transformational power of nature.
You can buy rocks and minerals c at specialty shops, but if you are on a budget, then you do not need to be worried. You can simply gather them on your own as a part of your practice. To do this, search for agates and jaspers on beaches and river beds. Then, proceed to look for signs of quartz, calcite, and other common minerals on public lands. The process is the most be-

autiful aspect of this.

Live Plants

Live plants have a way of adding health and vitality to any space. Thus, expecting their vibrancy at altars is not a mere wish. Get yourself a green thumb, place one or two small plants on your altar; they will breathe life and oxygen into your practice.

Use succulents and air plants if your altar is situated at a place it gets sufficient light, succulents These two types are preferred because of their small size and low maintenance requirements. To get a small plant, go to the nearest plant shops or ask people around you that are into horticulture.

Dried Herbs, Flowers, and Plants

Dried herbs and plants may be used in a variety of spells, rituals, and offerings, so keeping a selection on hand is always a good idea. Wander through natural areas and keep an eye out for useful herbs like rosemary and mint. These can be placed in your chalice or cauldron and left for a few days to dry. Hang gathered flowers upside down to dry, then place them on your altar for decoration and as a nod to the current season.

Animal Remains

When outside gathering materials for some of your other altar items, watch out for the remains of fallen animals. Look out for such things as bones, shed ant-

lers, teeth, fur. These things can be found where these
animals have chosen as an abode and have lost their
lives.

However, if you are intent on getting them at all cost,
then wooded areas in public lands away from main
trails should be where you are headed. Animal remains
can really the best altar adornment you need because
of the energy of nature's diverse array of life and the
way it reminds one of the certainties of death. Yet, you
need to know your state and country laws before hea-
ding out because some countries find it illegal to sca-
venge the remains of some protected species.

Jewelry

You can also include Jewelry. There are various things
you can add, like amulets, rings, brooches, and other
adornments. To get the best connection to them, try to
opt for the ones gifted to you by your family. This can
easily make powerful additions to your magical arse-
nal. Also, when you place jewels, you cherish you are
making it more personal, and adding a degree of ele-
gance to its aesthetic.

Crafts and Drawings

Because creation is such an aspect of magic, you can
include things you drew, painted, sculpted, assembled,
or otherwise. You can also make periodical changes of
your altar if you are an artist or one that creates things frequently. If you like, you can simply display older

pieces for the reconnection of forgotten times or feelings.

In case you have not created any real thing, you can
use this opportunity to make one of the classic altar
tools like the wand, broom, or pentacle.

Any Other Thing You Want To Include
When it comes to the assemblage and decoration of
your altar, there are no rules, so feel absolutely free to
include anything and everything not mentioned in this
list, so long as it contributes to your altar in one of the
following ways:
•   It gives you a reason to enjoy spending time at
your altar.
•   It personalizes your altar.
•   It helps in the direction of your energy or intention.
•   It has a significant function in your life or
practice.
•   It enables you to focus on your goals.
Here is a list of things you might want to include.

Representations of deities

You can place things like pictures, candles, a statue,
etc. Now, if you are one that honors a single god, you
can put things that represent them there. But if you
enjoy worshiping multiple deities, merely lining up
their various symbols at the back of the altar will do
just fine.

Representations of the Elements

These things can be a small cluster between the symbols of the deities you are worshiping. Make the edges
of the altar be the chosen area.

For Air
A censer, fan, feather, etc. They are masculine elements and can be placed on the right.

For Earth
A bowl of salt, cornmeal, sand, etc. They are feminine elements and can be placed on the left, representing the goddesses.

For Fire
A candle, lava rock, electric candle, etc. Same as the air. It can be placed on the right edge of the altar.

For Water
A bowl of water, seashell, small mirror, etc. Just like the earth, it can be placed on the left side of the altar

This was

WICCA TOOLS FOR BEGINNERS

the First book in Wicca Altar and Tools Series.
Please be sure to check out the other 2 books from the
same series.

WICCA ALTAR FOR BEGINNERS

WICCA SYMBOLS FOR BEGINNERS

Please consider leaving a great
5-Star review for this book

CPSIA information can be obtained
at www.ICGtesting.com
Printed in the USA
BVHW071225181120
593625BV00001B/229